CW00369910

Poems on Pr

An anthology of verse

by members of the

Society of Medical Writers

Editors

Mary Anderson, Joanne Regan and Chris Walker

http://www.somw.org.uk

Published by
the Society of Medical Writers

© Copyright contributors 2012

ISBN: 978-0-9573575-0-1

A CIP catalogue record for this book is available
from the British Library

Further copies obtainable from SOMW
c/o 1 Ballbrook Avenue, Manchester M20 6AB
maryanderson@btinternet.com
Telephone: 07887 984 266

Printed in the UK by RAP Spiderweb, Oldham, Lancs. UK
Cover illustration by Mike Walker http://www.mikeywalker.net

Poems on Prescription

CONTENTS

INTRODUCTION

The Society of Medical Writers is pleased to present this anthology of poems. All contributors are in some way connected with the medical world.

Some of the poems are serious and deal with life and death situations which regularly occur in health care settings. Perhaps they will give some insight into the emotional impact on the writer on these occasions. To give a little light relief some of the poems are amusing or tell of leisure activities. One section deals with situations which are heartbreaking and tell of the results of conflict activities including requests for asylum. 'Going for Gold' celebrates exercise and evokes the 2012 Olympics. The poem about the Brontë family was written for our autumn conference in Haworth. We believe that together the anthology makes a fascinating read and there is something for everyone.

We hope you will enjoy reading it.

The Society of Medical Writers was preceded by the General Practice Writers Association, renamed after it was decided to invite hospital doctors, students, nurses and other health care professionals to join us. This broadening of the membership has enhanced the activities of the society.

Dorothy Crowther
Chairman,
SOMW 2012

FLOOR PLAN FOR THE LIFE-CYCLE DEPARTMENT STORE

entrance

  layette
  baby clothes
  teddy bears
     school backpack
     bike
     sneakers
       skateboard
       video games
       hooded sweats
         wedding list
         wine rack
         appliances
           gardening tools
           golf clubs
           treadmill
             blood pressure cuff
             optometrist
             hearing aids
               cane
               walker
               wheelchair
                 shroud

                   exit

Norbert Hirschorn

ANONYMOUS

A new-born held in loving arms,
a child protected from all harm,
a pupil taught to do her best,
a daughter told to clean up her mess.

A best friend, who's loyal and true,
a familiar face whom everyone knew,
a big sister quick to forgive,
a young student, ready to live.

A first date, witty and smart,
a true love, with a big heart,
a new wife and a beautiful bride,
a young mother, gushing with pride.

A diligent worker, always with a smile,
a friendly neighbour, going the extra mile,
a wise nana with wisdom to share,
a faithful companion to whom none could compare.

And although that woman is gone,
her generous legacy will continue to live on.
She gave herself as a gift, selflessly,
to guide, teach and educate me.

Ruth Trimble
medical student

THE NEWBORN

Labour
They said
Is very hard.
And they were right.

The room rocks with emotion
It prickles, and explodes.
There is somehow
A change of light.

We hold our breath
And wait
And then we hear
That first cry
As she struggles into air.

Through that dark passage
That cave, that door.
From the mysteries of birth
To the mysteries of life.

Charmian Goldwyn

---

*Author's note: I was an observer in the process of getting
myself 'on the books' for providing antenatal care.*

BEGINNING IN INDIA AND ENGLAND

She lay inside a room with other girls
A curtain and a few short steps away.
She did not want those girls to hear her screams
But found she had to do it anyway.

It's hard to realise, when you're in pain
That everything's all right, though you've been told
That pain's a natural part of giving birth
Especially when you're just nineteen years old.

Her husband and her parents lie outside
On little mats that they have brought from home.
The wall between them feels like several miles
Never before has she felt so alone.

Earlier on, her father was sent out
The doctor made him go to buy some blood.
He took an auto rickshaw round the town
And went to every hospital he could.

He came back empty handed and dismayed
It's 3 am and thirty-nine degrees.
There's nothing left for him to do but wait
And offer prayers to Allah on his knees.

At last, the baby comes into the world
The midwife brings the infant to the door.
The men go home, but grandma stays behind
Her place is on the lying-in ward's floor

The nurses will give special care and drugs
The female relatives must do the rest
So other mothers sleep within the ward
On blankets underneath their children's beds.

But, back in England, there's a girl
With all the care we can provide
A clean bed, medics all on hand
And mum and husband by her side.

The midwife's reassuring voice
Calms down the worried spouse and mum
"This anger's just another phase.
That means that labour's nearly done"

She feels frustrated, hot and cross.
There's no way she can stop the pain
Like every woman in her place
She swears not to do this again.

It's over and the baby's out
The midwife puts him to her breast
Her husband cheers, her mother cries,
Her worst day now becomes her best.

Although we know we can improve
We're thankful for the NHS.
That little girl in India
Is managing on so much less.

Chris Walker

THE HOSPITAL

Hope

It is being in hospital one sunny day
Waiting and hoping for the doctor to say
Everything is fine, you're going home today

Despair

It is being in hospital one sunny day
You've been tested and rested
You wait for an answer
The doctor then says
"By the way, you have cancer"

Joy

It is being in hospital one sunny day
After nine months' confinement the time has arrived
The wife is in place with a contorted face
Nothing can stop it no matter what
Is it a girl or is it a boy?
Twelve hours later arrives your bundle of joy
A lifetime of pleasure with your little treasure
Leaving the hospital one sunny day

Joanne Regan

MY BABY LIVES

There's a bloody bandage round his fist
Electrodes on his chest and wrist
And tubes from every orifice
Who cares? My baby lives.

He doesn't like it on the ward
His body's weak, his breathing's flawed
He's in pain, miserable and bored
Who cares? My baby lives.

I've got to go, without a doubt
The hospital has let him out
The train fare's closed my bank account
Who cares? My baby lives.

It's full of crowds in London town
Police cars screeching up and down
There's stifling heat and deafening sound
Who cares? My baby lives.

He's got a long scar down his chest
His ribs are showing through his vest
He looks thin even when he's dressed
Who cares? My baby lives.

He's filled the saucepans up with sticks
And dropped the car keys from a bridge
He's throwing food out of the fridge
Sweet joy! My baby lives!

Chris Walker

ELLIE'S SEVEN MINUTES WITH THE GP

This hapless child of twenty-one
Now has four babes in a tiny flat.
Damp, she says, and the mould's begun
To spoil the bed of their feral cat;
And her partner's taken to sullen withdrawal
Which festers and simmers to a violent expression
In her purple bruises and painful crawl
To a respectable refuge they call depression.

Her oldest's autistic and will not talk;
The twins' ADHD * talks too much:
Propels them to run before they can walk;
And a prem caesarean has added to her clutch.
This latest maternal and foetal distress
Could easily have caused Ellie and her baby to die.
"I know," she said, "that my life's a mess,"
"But I love babies," she smiled, "so that's why."

Ray Hume

---

*ADHD - Attention Deficit Hyperactivity Disorder

JOURNEYMAN

Feral youth leaving home
Old enough to be on his own
With his mates he takes a ride
On the tracks, but which side?

Edgy, inquisitive
To see how others live
Ready for adventure
Without parental censure

Finding out for himself
Trying to make sense
Of what his eyes will see
And just who he might be

With his brothers in arms he plays it cool
In far off cities will he be temptation's fool?
Fears and sensitivities concealed
Only when a man will they be revealed

I miss him, even the teenage attitude
I can see he's a pretty cool dude.
As the wheels turn along the track
My son, who will be coming back?

Jim Brockbank

HALLELUJAH AT SIXTY

1. Some say at sixty I'm pretty cool
   Others say I'm just an old fool
   Now my friends you don't believe that do you
   I've made it through to decade seven
   My pension's through and I'm in heaven
   My pass to freedom Glory Hallelujah!
   Hallelujah, hallelujah, hallelujah, hallelujah

2. In decade one I went to school
   I talked in class and I played the fool
   The teacher said, you just don't listen do you
   I tried to pay attention more
   In the eleven plus I made the score
   My Mother cried and called out Hallelujah!
   Hallelujah, hallelujah, hallelujah, hallelujah

3. In decade two, the teenage years
   I muddled through my hopes and fears
   With attitude I tried to sock it to you
   But girls were scarce and dates were rare
   I learned to shave and grow my hair
   But then I scored, and Glory Hallelujah!
   Hallelujah, hallelujah, hallelujah, hallelujah

4. In decade three my student days
   My first degree all in a haze
   You don't expect me to remember do you?
   I studied and I played it hard
   Held student life in high regard
   Went back for more, Glory Hallelujah!
   Hallelujah, hallelujah, hallelujah, hallelujah

5. My life it changed in decade four
   I met the girl that I adore
   Should come as no surprise to you
   They call me Lucky Jim
   That December night my luck was in
   And every breath I drew was Hallelujah!
   Hallelujah, hallelujah, hallelujah, hallelujah

6. We moved to Hampton Hill
   It seemed that the whole world was ill
   They'd queue around the corner just to see you
   And I became a family man
   Trying to do the best I can
   The boys were born, Glory Hallelujah!
   Hallelujah, hallelujah, hallelujah, hallelujah

7. The millennium years, the kids they grew
   And we made good friends too
   You never do get the work-life balance do you?
   But I've no reason for feeling blue
   I've got my pension through
   A pass to freedom Glory Hallelujah!
   Hallelujah, hallelujah, hallelujah, hallelujah

Jim Brockbank

Sung by a GP with his guitar on his 60th birthday, to the tune of Leonard Cohen's 'Hallelujah'.

DESPERADO

1. Desperado now that I'm sixty
   I just ain't so nifty I need to take care
   I'm getting older now, I've got to accept that
   although it's grey at least I've still got my hair
   Now I can't pee straight and time won't wait,
   I've got a bad back and my muscles all ache,
   and I can't remember where I parked the car.
   My eyesight's dim and my body ain't so trim
   I'm beginning to think that life's a bit grim
   and I wonder if I am a fading star.

2. Desperado I ain't getting no younger my ulcer
   gives me hunger pains I try to relieve
   Rest up now, take it easy, I put on some make up
   in an effort to deceive
   Now my feet get cold in the winter time
   I've a midlife crisis and my hair don't shine,
   and it's hard to tell the night time from the day
   My blood pressure's high and I'm feeling low
   and now I've got a hernia down below
   and I recognise the symptoms of decay.

3. Desperado don't feel too sad, it ain't so bad
   they all tell me. I'll never be alone,
   I've got Helen and the boys at home
   they've promised to pamper and look after me.
   Now I've got my pension through
   there's no reason for feeling blue,

I'll go fly-fishing and catch myself a trout
If I feel that life has passed me by,
and when asked my age of course I lie,
don't worry there's a lot of it about.

4. Desperado, I really don't think so,
   I don't get my spirits low
   I only jest
   Becoming sixty is no big deal,
   you're only as old as you feel
   Now my song is over I'm off to have a rest!

Jim Brockbank

Sung by Jim on his 60th birthday, to the tune of 'Desperado' by The Eagles

ALONENESS

Visiting the cottage
I held the key.
Gently I walked in
To the elderly kitchen.

I watched
Through the back window.
There was peace about her eyes
As she pottered in the garden.

Picking here a weed
A dead flower head.
Watching the birds
Around the crumbs.

Such peace.

She looked up
And saw me through the window.
At once the anxious wrinkles flew back.
"Come in, a cup of tea?"

Eager to please
To hear the news.
The quiet moment gone.
Her aloneness
Waiting

For me to go.

Charmian Goldwyn

ONE HUNDRED TODAY

The balloons say it, the cards say it,
One hundred today, what a fuss!
Lots of post and a card from the Queen,
Visitors galore, family and friends,
Many people I haven't seen
For years and years and years

Three parties and three cakes,
Can't keep up
So much attention, never had it before
Not once in a hundred years,
But it's rather nice.

The mayor comes and
I hold his chains as we talk
Of trams and gas lamps and
Other things from the past
The good old days, all the things I remember.

Go to church, take communion. I stand up
And everyone sings Happy Birthday,
They all seem to know me.
How is that? It's only my birthday.
The last I hope and expect
So I'll enjoy every minute.

Dorothy Crowther

Author's note: A tribute to my mother-in law, Gertrude Crowther
13th Oct 1906 - 30th Dec 2006. To the end a very lively lady.

A SWALLOW OF COURSE

"And what do you see?" asked the priest
fearing the wind from the east,
holding the old woman's hand.
"A crocus," she said, without raising her head,
"A crocus in blue and a snowdrop or two,
and buds on the tree.
That is what I can see."

"And what do you hear?" asked the nurse
fearing the wind from the north,
holding the old woman's hand.
"A bleating," she said, without raising her head,
"and the bells, and their peals, and the sheep
in the fields, and the rustling of deer.
That is what I can hear."

"And what can you smell?" they both asked,
fearing the wind from the south,
holding the old woman's hands.
"All April," she said, without raising her head,
"and the daffodils spent by the gales in Lent,
and the ferns on the fell.
That is what I can smell."

"And what can you taste?" asked the rest,
fearing the wind from the west,
all holding the old woman's hands.
"Some honey," she said, without raising her head,
"and the mint in the tea, and the salt from the sea,
and the sharpness of haste.
That is what I can taste."

"From the psalmist a song, for a wafer the tongue,
for the wine that will follow,
for the bread that you swallow . . . "
"And for the spring," said the rest
for they were the guests.

But autumn had come, dismissing the sun.
"A swallow?" she said, without raising her head.
"Yes . . . a swallow of course. And the swallows."

Richard Cutler

OUR DEAR BROTHER

He was sitting upright in his high-back chair.
His eyes were unmoving but he seemed to smile.
"We don't know what's wrong
But he sits so still,"
Said the two sisters, clutching their hands.
They may have known but they would not tell.
When I said what it was
One brushed away a tear,
Pushed it away with the back of her hand.
Then quietly they stood, taking it in.
Living together for so many years
How could it all just end in tears?
But he had left them a message
And that was his smile.
As I walked from the house I glanced at my watch.
It was eight in the morning.
Beyond the fragility was something deeper.
Tears tell of a timeless mystery.
Human loneliness is but a fear of life.
We look at the sea and feel a beating heart.

Tony Spalding

THE MOMENT

When we first met she was writing a letter.
She only had a few days to live
And I threw away all her pills.
Days later her breathing became laboured.
I sat beside her and she took my hand,
While her husband stood by the dresser.
Her grip became firmer and then she was gone,
And we were only two in the silent room.
Something then happened, unexpected.
There was a sense of another with us,
Not seen, not heard, but there,
Concerned, insightful, knowing.
At the garden gate it faded.
It seemed a timeless moment,
Not forgotten, that dying,
And that presence that consoled.

Tony Spalding

TEN FEET TALL

Ten years on and I miss him
The sensitivity behind the wry smile
The clothes sense and the importance of style
Better than mine, but then I was Lucky Jim.
The holidays we might have had,
back to Corfu or Rhodes I wouldn't have cared
The dappled sunlight, a cool beer, voyeurs of our children
  growing up
Lazy talk of matters of import, even a post-mortem
  of the FA Cup
Moments of silence except the holiday sounds, shared

"So what do you think, does that seem O.K?"
Talking together on the phone, at home, or while having
  some grub
Playing football with the kids in the summer garden
  of the pub
"Rick, can I meet you after work, the White Cross or
  the Victoria Inn? I've had a difficult day."

He was occasionally stubborn, always determined and
  always right
But luck was to play a part and I had it all.
In luck I was a giant ten feet tall.
Rick's share of luck was cruelly small

In celebration of his life the church was packed to
  the rafters
Reminiscence of the St Cuthbert's childhood years
  as choirboys together

Friday night choir practice whatever the weather.
A celebration of achievement and courage, but what
   lies after?

After lies what might have been
The midlife questions a fiftieth birthday together
Lazy talk of import, 'our kids they seem quite clever'
My wish list of topics for him, in my dreams

In courage instead of luck, he had it all
The searing incurable illness from which he died
Revealed a battle of will that filled me with pride
He was a giant of a man my twin brother Rick, ten feet tall.

Jim Brockbank
2002

6th APRIL

It's an out of step sort of a day
Unpaired
Like a lost sock or a missing glove.

The blues, out of rhythm
Just off the beat
Now twenty years on, and I still miss him.

Ducks not quite in a row
They will be
But not today, it's Our Birthday.

Jim Brockbank
2012

BASRA WALL, NEWS AT TEN

The middle-aged mother
Kissed her right index finger,
Shut her eyes tight in pain,
Pressed the pulp of her loving tender
Finger onto the cold shiny
Brass plaque on the warm red brick.

It all started so very differently,
In a bright white room on the
Top floor of the maternity block
With the smell of Hibiscrub, amniotic fluid and apprehension.
We smiled as he was bundled into
A white Terry Towel.
Our love and our hopes
Were with him; our fears too.

Later, in a Khaki cauldron
Devoid of cool, calm or colour,
Death was sent quickly to his head,
Or at least that's what his mother knows.

He was nearly famous for a minute.
Standards dipped in honour,
In a middle English town,
On the ten o'clock news.

Now only his mother
With her atrophy can kiss her right index finger,
Shut her eyes tight in pain,
Press the pulp of her loving
Finger onto the cold shiny
Brass plaque, on the warm red brick.

Keith Tattum – 2010

A WALK IN THE PARK

You are a beautiful soul
So close to our hearts
The Thames ran swiftly for you
The blossom was on the trees
Light cloud and blue skies held off the rain for you
And we walked in celebration of you

Jim Brockbank

*Author's note: on the recent death from meningitis of a young
student friend.*

THE BRONTË FAMILY

The children, five girls and one boy,
all blessed with brilliant minds,
lived in Haworth, with their Irish rector father
and their Cornish mother, a happy household.

Cancer took their mother,
a deep and unforgettable tragedy.
Aunt Branwell came to live, giving
as much love as she was able.
But a mother can never be replaced.

A reputable school for daughters of the clergy
was cruel and offered poor conditions,
insufficient food and bad sanitation.
Maria then Elizabeth died of tuberculosis:
TB was to be the family scourge.

Schooldays were over:
Father could risk no more deaths in his family.
They learnt at home, created stories
of *Angria* and *Gondal* in tiny books
which no-one else could read.

They explored the surrounding moors and
honed the stories and poems which were in their minds.
The atmosphere of the graveyard in front of the house
the wildness of the world beyond, their own hardships all
acted as catalysts in the creative process.
Was their writing a therapeutic release?

When visiting Haworth you begin to understand the
feelings of Cathy in *Wuthering Heights,*
and appreciate the complexity of Heathcliff.

Emily drank in the wildness of the moors.
She and *Keeper* her dog visited *Top Withens,* isolated
    farmhouse.
Was it here that *Wuthering Heights* was born?

In *Jane Eyre*, Charlotte depicts conditions in the school
    where her sisters died,
and the life of the lonely governess in a Gothic Manor.
Was its creation a sop to her own sadness?
Did it help her to come to terms with her losses?
Was it cathartic? Did the writing help her, even
    subconsciously?

In *The Tenant of Wild Fell Hall,*
Anne, the early feminist, brings out the horror and isolation
    of marital abuse.
Her vivid imagination was fed by observation
And memories of her own pain and loss.

Branwell took to drink and cocaine.
His legendary nights at the Black Bull together with
Tuberculosis killed him and his creative talent.
His artistic abilities remained untapped.
Did self-deprecation make him remove himself from
the family portrait which now shows only his sisters?

The imagination and harsh experiences of this family
produced some of the greatest writings
in the English language.

Their own story is even more amazing.
Sadly they all died young
but through their books they will live for ever.

Dorothy Crowther

Author's note: Mrs Brontë died of cancer, and five of her children died of TB. Charlotte died of pneumonia during pregnancy. Today all would have lived. Would they have produced more great works? Only the father lived on. We hear nothing of his anguish. Although he was helped by Charlotte's husband he must surely have been devastated by the loss of all his family.

LIFE INTERRUPTED

It's a mass of humanity
That's what she said
We must embrace them
But now she's dead

Spent her life Consulting
Knowing what's best
Hanging on her every word
None of them had guessed

Looking splendid in shoes & suit
She played a glamorous game
A lifetime of knowledge lost
When the cancer came again

Compassion became a chore
Once the mass erupted
Hanging on through pain
Doctor's life, interrupted

Joanne Regan

THE VERY IMPORTANT LADY DOCTOR

Oh dear I'm so important to all and sundry, patients dear.
They need me every moment to consult and to be near.
My Partners need me too, to have a laugh and have a groan
Receptionists to give advice, to sign a script and take
   the phone.
The Manager is seeking me to sign a cheque and fill a form.
The Midwife wants to tell me more how little Frank
   was born.
The Health Visitor is waiting to tell of Frank's poor
   mother more:
A really squalid bedsit and a high depression score.
The cleaner wants me now as she really must get in
To hoover up the floor and empty out the bin.
The Practice Nurse is waiting quietly in the wings
"Please take blood from Mr Smith and check a few
   small things."
The District Nurse is sighing,"Have you not seen
   Mabel yet?
Her blisters have all burst and the bed is soaking wet!"

Now the Chemist's on the line with a query on a script.
I feel as if my brain into treacle has been dipped.
The Secretary's waiting – she can't understand my tape.
I really must be clearer when my letters I dictate.

On line 2 waits Social Services with an urgent "if I will?"
"Please come now and see Jack Rogers at his house
with the Old Bill." They're there to try and help
   as poor Jack's gone quite A.W.O.L.

They're worried if they leave him he'll be at risk and hence
    the call.
They think I must assess him now; a Section 3 might
    be required.
Has anybody noticed? . . . The doctor's getting tired.

Thirty coffees later, several smiles and several groans
A very tired doctor will make her own way home.
And there at home she'll find four men await her too
But with love and understanding to help her make
    it through
The sadness and the upsets that her fellow humans bring
To her as "their doctor" be they patient, foe or friend.
And so the day is over, just one day in one long life,
The doctor turns to mother then to cleaner, cook and wife.
And she wonders if each day if one human heart
    she's touched,
Then all the aggravations will have been worth
    so very much.

Karen O'Reilly

THE TREE OF LIFE

I swear to fulfil, to the best of my ability and judgement,
 this covenant:

Permit yourself to lose your mind,
To wander through the mist in mine,
To experience my thoughts and instincts too,
And find yourself respect, anew.

Fall to your knees and kiss the ground,
Where your elders' elders' feet are found.
You walk their walk in brand new shoes,
Their hard earned work, they toil, you cruise.
So teach your children how to stroll,
As one day they will pay the toll,
But hope yourself, and hold your sigh,
That the price they pay is not so high.

Imagine your patients as boats at sea,
Where you yourself will play the breeze,
You push too hard, the boat will sway,
Yet puff too little, they go astray.

Never let yourself forget,
We're all with nature, one regret,
That you think yourself of iron heart,
And so, observe your soul depart.
For when travellers feel the end is nigh,
They sense around them, the cost is high,
So show them now what love you can,
For their Doctor too, should be of man.

Bellow for help when lost in the wood,
As though hailing the stars, as if you could,
For when the darkness comes and you're finally beat,
It's too late now to halt defeat.
If the path ahead is known by a friend,
Then lend him your map to mark and to mend,
As it's not just your duty, but your privilege too,
To be shown the way home, if the pathway is new.

Know that your patient is much like white sand,
Precious and peaceful, so please understand,
That their truths are not yours to allow for release,
For they belong to the patient, let the beach lie in peace.
But pick up your spade and always dig deep,
There is treasure down there, though not yours to keep,
But the bounty will help in passing the day,
And the care of your patient, so do not delay.

You've found them while searching the great unknown,
Where there are brand new birds they do not know
    have flown,
Just remember when showing them how the forest
    has grown
That very few travellers walk it alone.
There are brothers and sisters and whole families sick,
They're aware that it's grim, death missed by a lick,
And so give them your word that you're not just there
    to mend,
But to show them that home will continue to fend.

Tell them their adventure is one to admire,
Inform them that wisdom is a worthy desire,
But if you can give them just one thing to lay on their lap,
To keep them out of the woods – please give them a map.

And so make promises to read this when approaching
   the green,
Know the wind and the rain are just part of the scene,
You should know, as I do, that this land is of strife,
But I'll protect it with passion, the great tree of life.

Sean Cassidy
medical student

---

*Editor's note: At their medical school (Dundee) these students have been
encouraged to reflect on the Hippocratic Oath and write a new version..*

MORE THAN A JOB

As a doctor I will hold firm to my faith,
Your life is a gift given and taken by God,
You are more than a number, more than a name,
You are my equal, **you** deserve my help.

We'll work together on this,
Our relationship will be built on honesty, confidentiality
   and trust,
And I will do my best to help and not harm **you.**

I will endeavour to know my own limits,
To continue to grow and mature as a physician,
To never give up.

I will remind myself daily why I chose this career,
Rekindle the passion for helping those in need.

My duty is to **you**, my patient,
Your quality of life, **your** wishes.

Kathryn McCullough
medical student

DEAFENING SILENCE

Struck by an immense anticipation,
I step into the slumbering ward.
The deafening silence.
The voices of their past,

The voices of their loved ones,
Echoing in my mind,
As I walk through this unique academy,
Toward my Tutor and Guide.

" . . . You've gone; you've left an aching void,
Where once you poured in joy.
A life of memories forever I shall cherish,
My dear husband . . ."

I venture through this maze,
The quickening rhythm of a beating heart,
The blood coursing through veins,
I pass a Tutor and Guide.

Surrounded by pupils,
Their eyes fixed upon the unveiling of his secrets;
By my side I hear fragments of praises,
Sung out into Eternity by hearts so dear,

" . . . Much more than my companion,
Far more than my source of help;
My comforter in days of sorrow,
My beloved wife . . ."

The emotion and the emotionless,
Thoughts racing and heart pounding.
" . . . I will miss you so much,
My dear Grampa . . ."
Proceeding past these precious teachers,
These instructors of invaluable worth,
I approach my personal Tutor,
My very own Guide.

I hear the devotions and hymns of adoration,
Of those who knew my cherished Guide,
Such praises rising from the hearts and souls,
Of loved ones so dear,

Too poignant, too sacred to put into words,
The cries of those who adored you,
Whose lives you touched in Time,
The very hearts that carry you for Eternity.

Gareth Carmichael
medical student

DEATH AND THE CADAVER

Walking into the room I sensed my own mortality
We soon met our cadaver with a degree of formality
Peeling back the cover I felt close to fainting
The figure beneath as still as a painting
She was stripped of all life, memory and vanity
But I guess I still worry that I'll lose my humanity
A small white cloth was placed round her head
To make it easier to touch the cold metal bed

On the first day I didn't make an incision
But since then I've changed my decision
My peers have helped me more than I can say
And I find myself cutting a little deeper each day
So I think I've learned more from my body
Than from books on a shelf
Not just about anatomy but also myself

Ian Hyndman
medical student

FUGUE

minutes, hours, a day?
Sore, sodden feet
carry a beleaguered mind
fed by onion and chips
dry blood, circulates
while you cannulate [1]
again, again, again
bleep, bleep, bleep
an incessant alarm
that never signals dawn
natural light
glimpses fleeting
fluorescent jaundice
coats the body
call ends when day breaks
fresh dawn, fresh air
invigorates, briefly
blurs of a commute home
punctuated with amber, red, green
no falling water to cleanse a mind
as horizontal cotton closes over
waves of exhaustion
repeat, mane. [2]

Paul Dhillon

---

1. *Cannulate - insert cannula (wide needle) into a patient's artery or vein.*
2. *Mane -'in the morning'; often a medication instruction.*

METAMORPHOSIS
or TRAVELS WITH A STETHOSCOPE

Through a narrow plastic pipe a conduit to another world
familiar to the white tailed
senses shrunken down to one
in this theatre I'm all ears
where nothing is no more than sound.

A rumble of thunder only the unnoticed parting of clothes
somewhere else for I am here
deep in a high summer meadow
busy with life's invisible movings
and faraway borborygmi

distant traffic occasionally near. The unseeing
   visitor listens
to a gentle vesicular breeze
flowing through grass and rustling leaves
like a swimmer aware of regular breathing
now in water the smallest of noises

darts into earshot. Sounds can't be placed.
Heavier mysteries out of sight
deeper lie hints of tectonic shifts
all in an aquarium.
A mist descends as if night has fallen.
I strain to hear what should be heard.

A crepitation, cracking sticks, rhonchi, perhaps
   a pleural creak
some ancient door drawing to
on its own. Here are hums
and murmurs where streams' disturbance
creates new sound when you are blind.

Bats fly by like half heard words whispering pectoriloquy
vocal resonance returning
unexpected recollections of a coin
thoughtfully dropped
into the depths of the well

dead of night approaches so the alien leaves before all sounds
   are lost
through time and space and narrow tubes
dizzy from travel I emerge to see
if I can grasp the phrases for those who wait
for me to resume my shape and senses.

Richard Westcott

NIGHT STAFF

She gives me back my self respect;
Changes the bed that I have wet;
Bathes me so I'm cool again;
Treats me gently, easing pain.
She is from abroad
sending money home
for her children she has not seen
these two-three years,
and is living here alone.

Mary Anderson

MISSING THE POINT

You saw your elder sister when she died,
and asked me later why her wrinkles disappeared
and why she looked so young again.
Not wanting to fail
I tried to answer as best I could.
'Blah blah . . . collagen fibres . . . postmortem changes'
I broke the silence, filling space with words,
pesudo-science, verbiage,
and felt I'd done it rather well.

It was only afterwards . . .

Mary Anderson

44

REMEMBERING TALKING TO A BEREAVED RELATIVE

You sit. I sit.
We talk.
And my other voice says, "I know".

We sit.
You talk.
I listen.
And my other voice says, "I know".

I know you hurt.

You sit
And talk. I sit
And listen.
And feel.

And my other voice falls silent.

I hurt.

My pain. Unseen.

The silent voice within
Is calm.

Your tears. Your pain. My hurt.

Karen O'Reilly

ADVICE
or LESS TO SAY

Healing is for old men
young man do not go there
wait till you have less to say
and can leave alone
both ill and well to
go their way
as will you
                so wait
till you have less to say
and have grown old
then you can hope
to understand
even heal
                you will
become an old man
in your own time
young man
                go there then
when there is more
though you'll have less
to say.

Richard Westcott

TOUCH
or BREAKING GOOD NEWS

Double click . . . wait.
Electrons shift.
Glaring back flat panorama to concavity,
to convex, to convoluted.

Waiting. Hoping. Negativity
Is the positive.

Normal range.

Peristaltic waves of relief
Inside. You.

Dead epidermis, connects with sloughing necrosis
of another.
Death conceals the living
heat.

Warmth transmits, across – against death.

Verbal echoes.
Normal.

Paul Dhillon

---

*Author's note: on finding a normal result on the computer and giving
the patient the good news.*

THE SHAMAN

The timid woman
collects her courage
and visits the Shaman for
help with her disfigurement.

She enters in
with fear and humility.

The Great Shaman
rests a hand on her shoulder
and heals her pain.

She leaves uplifted
with courage and strength.

Disfigured still
but beautiful.

Alive in the sunlight.

And the Shaman?
Cloistered in the darkness
of his healing room.

He sits alone
looking out.

All powerful.
All knowing.

Saved only by the absence of a looking-glass.

Karen O'Reilly

LIFE FORCE

Life force, bright colours of sound
Light up, as I pass the school playground.
Spirit lifts:
Young lives, vital gifts.

Make ready for the daily processional
Ebb and flow of the clinical confessional:
A place of privilege in ordinary lives
Takes its toll on both sides.

Black news, white shadow, crimson cough–
This telling cannot be put off–
He comes through the door.
Defeated eyes transfixed to the floor.

Empathy spills across the room.
Struggle to lighten the message of doom
Fast track referral–the two week rule–
Be honest. He's no fool.

Next patient please, sings the digital screen.
The emotional slate must wipe itself clean.

Next patient please. Undercurrents remain
Cradled by the pulse of the playground refrain.

Jim Brockbank

THE GIRL FROM ADSWOOD

I'm just a girl from Adswood who grew up and then grew old.
But I had a great career as a nurse.
I wasn't the best student, in fact I was the worst.
Thank goodness, after me they broke the mould.

I ran out of starchy aprons and my frilly cap fell off.
I did my homework in the pub and never did enough.
My tights were always wrinkled, no two legs looked
   the same.
If Nora Batty'd seen them, she'd have had to raise her game.
But my ever patient tutors made a nurse of me in time,
The only one to stay the course among my class of nine.

I made it as a midwife, and women stop to say,
"Hey, you delivered so and so, you were kind to me that day".
They say, "You must remember me, I so remember you."
And usually I really don't, but just pretend I do.
I'm caught out when they say to me "Well, you were
   pregnant too.
I had a ten pound bouncing boy. Was that what you had, too?"
As I have had both boys and girls, I haven't got a clue
So I say, "A lovely baby! Was it the same for you?"

My greatest challenge was the care of disadvantaged groups.
I worked so hard to keep them well and bring them in the loop.
When I had solved their problems and their aches and pains
   were gone,
They would try to keep in touch and I was everybody's mum.

When I retired, my party was a treasure to behold
For all the people that I'd helped dressed up and came in
  droves.
I didn't want to leave them, it was just my time to go.
I was ready for a rest, if only for a year or so.

The shyest person sang for me, the first time she'd been bold
To me, that simple song was like a little bit of gold
So many people loved me, it was humbling to be told
'Cos, I'm just a girl from Adswood, who grew up, and then
  grew old.

Chris Walker

SONG FOR SUE

Sue's been at the Practice for thirty years and more
There's nothing in the NHS she hasn't seen before
She's the Queen of QoF [1], she reigned over the Red Book [2]
She spared nothing in the effort that she took

She maximised our income, she promoted patient care
The Practice goes to pot whenever she's not there
We gather in a huddle, we don't know what to do
We just can't face the day without our Super Sue

Chorus
   So Sue we thank you, for all that you have done
   Of Julian's pension, we think you should get a share
   That he gets it all, just don't seem fair
   We've organised the payments direct to you
   A Direct Debit to Super Sue
   In thirty years we've had a lot of fun
   Thank you from our hearts for all that you have done

Sue came to Park Road in 1982
What she was getting into she didn't have a clue
There were no performance indicators and no IT
No Darzi, No Roadmap, and No PCT [3]

Fundholding was yet to rise and fall
By the year 2000 Sue thought she'd seen it all
Politicians don't understand the NHS, she would scoff
Then along came the new contract and a thing called QoF

---

1. QoF: Quality and Outcomes Framework
2. The Red Book: NHS Statement of Fees and Allowances
3. PCT: Primary Care Trust

Chorus

> *So Sue we thank you, for all that you have done*
> *Of Julian's pension, we think you should get a share*
> *That he gets it all, just don't seem fair*
> *We've organised the payments direct to you*
> *A Direct Debit to Super Sue*
> *In thirty years we've had a lot of fun*
> *Thank you from our hearts for all that you have done*

But nothing was to phase Sue or threaten her resolve
There didn't seem to be a problem that she couldn't solve
LES, extended hours, or services to enhance
She could do it all without a backward glance

Sue, we're going to miss you, more than we can say
Vince Cable has your number. You're a phone call away
From an invite to advise on the NHS;
"Sue, we need an expert who can sort out this mess"!

Chorus

> *So Sue we thank you, for all that you have done*
> *Of Julian's pension, we think you should get a share*
> *That he gets it all, just don't seem fair*
> *We've organised the payments direct to you*
> *A Direct Debit to Super Sue*
> *In thirty years we've had a lot of fun*
> *Thank you from our hearts for all that you have done*

Jim Brockbank

LAMENT FOR THE NATIONAL HEALTH SERVICE

I have to think they cannot understand
What they have done;
They cannot understand
What made us tick.
Perhaps they lack some vital cog
Like cripples with important bits missing.
I try to see that as their loss

But I can't.

I am too angry
I am too sad
They do not understand
That they have killed for me a deeply precious thing.

And they have cheaply flogged
Something that was ours
Without our leave
Having promised
Honest injun
That they never would.

But promises they made elsewhere
Have mattered more
Than ones they made to
Coarse proles on streets outside their Club
How could such people understand
What they have done.

The world's too full of greed,
Too full of hate,
Too full of deceit,

Too full of self-interest,
Too prostrate before the worthless rich
To have destroyed a thing so deeply good
Just because its warmth and wisdom
and the awkward fact of its success
Shamed
Those who denied the world could work this better way.

This balm for the new callousness
This moral for the new amorality
Had to be destroyed
Or they'd be proven wrong
These modern barons,
Pathetically locked in counting up their spoils

So, we must not let them once deny
the fact that it did work
Yes
For half a century it worked
This inspirational dream
Of far far greater men.
And, though they cannot understand what they have done,
That simple truth will live
Must live
To prove that they were wrong
All along.

James Willis

ZOO- AND JUNGLE-DOCTORS

The first prefer their patients kept in cages, labelled with
their name and symptoms, test results and diagnoses.
The latter are alert to stripey shadows and muffled grunts,
only seen and heard for seconds in the undergrowth.

The first are clad in white, and like to read the patient's notes,
examine – sometimes, ponder pompously, and then pronounce.
The latter harvest what they can from every fleeting chance,
to weave a diagnostic web from half guessed-at, random data.

The first lot gain from information carefully filed,
blood tests, scans – both ultrasound and MRI,
but lose out to the other sort by hardly knowing
who the patient is, and being lost without their notes;

whilst the latter thrive on knowing him, his family,
whose patterns of illness bequeathed, like relay batons,
down the line, can suggest an answer without much effort,
even in the environment of the jungle's screening dim.

Each would hate to do the other's work – and could not.
Temperament guides the choice of which is right for us,
and points the way without us knowing; as true for medics
   as for you and me.
Just let them be – Consultant and GP.

Chris Cameron

ABROAD THOUGHTS FROM HOME

My eyes have been looking at the far-off peaks
It's hard to concentrate on print again.
Beyond the page I see the mounds and crags,
Cascades, and tumbling stones and mountain streams.

You sit in my old patient's chair and speak to me
But past your body I am watching birds
Behind your head the clouds are sailing by
And round your feet I thought a lizard stirred.

I know you sit in my old patient's chair
Your troubles pouring out. But am I here?
My body may be, but my soul is there
Above the masses in the snow fresh air
Paused, leaning on my staff and gazing wide
As peak on peak upon horizon stride.

What, I'm not attending, you'll come another day?
But no! I heard it all dear patient stay . . .
"There's a lot of it about", I say.

Charmian Goldwyn

BILLY (MEDIC)

Billy,
It's thirty years
Since you cooked
Something con carne
And wore a yellow
Lampshade on your head,
In an institution
On the hill above the
Banks of the flooded
Sedgy Severn.
You never stopped laughing.

The next day,
A cold bland Sunday,
We walked along Stiper Stones.
Gliders skimmed the edge
And our heads,
And we laughed and
Drank to Prince Rupert
And Owen Glendower
And all those who were
Slaughtered near the Travel Inn
On the A53 roundabout.

We didn't see it Billy,
Your encroaching madness.
Your impending madness.
It crept onto us,
Perhaps even onto you,

Like the tide at Southport
Silently slipping towards the shore,
Trapping innocents like you.

Confirmation came,
If confirmation were ever needed,
At 3 am one cold January morning.
You rang me from Randolph's
In Oxford,
To tell me you were smoking Havanas (you hated smoking),
Drinking Dom Perignon,
And relishing your new appointment
As Bishop.

I stood on the cold concrete
Of the kitchen floor,
Knowing this was in many ways
The end, and at the same time,
Not even the beginning.

Keith Tattum

NICOLE KIDMAN IS COOKING MY TEA

Slope up is a lazy dog.
Flashy, dashy suntanny fab.
Never ever better!
Zingy zingy zingy zong.
There is absolutely nothing wrong,
Nicole Kidman is cooking my tea.

Top of the mountain.
Brighter than bright bright white.
Christ was never more witty.
I'm dancing on the table because its free, and
Nicole Kidman is cooking my tea.

Let's book a good holiday.
Move house, buy a car.
Buy a gazebo, a carpet, a freezer,
Four Xboxes, a Sony DVD
Nicole Kidman is cooking my tea.

Crisis team, prices team,
Somewhere inbetweeny team.
Butter nutter, nutter fucker.
Psychiatrists can take a joke.
Lithium is fandabifine by me.
Don't dare forget,
Nicole Kidman is cooking my tea.

Keith Tattum

FLOTSAM

You never know what may come and what may go
stuff gets washed away just when you thought
you wanted it now it's here but there it's gone
even as you wonder what it was you never know
something else floats by not what you thought
you had in mind still you never know it may be
useful no need to worry then if you thought
you lost it as the unexpected drifts in so
let the waters flow thoughts come and go
you never know how much you never know

Richard Westcott

THOUGHTS

Thoughts
around my head
Like leaves
Like raven's wings around my face
Whispering urgently
"Catch me! Catch me!"

I reach and catch
A holly leaf. It prickles me
Red speck of blood is on my palm.

I drop it, reach again
Into the whirling fluttering thoughts.
A dry leaf crumbles in my hand . . .
I crush it and a speck of dust
Sticks to the blood.

I watch it
Think to clean it with my cuff,
But as I watch it melts like snow
Leaving no mark.
My palm is clean.

I look around
The air is still
No threatening Leaf Wings
Anywhere.

The thoughts have gone.
Although I know, unbidden
That they may return.
Just now
The silence is wonderful to hear.

Charmian Goldwyn

THE CAN OF WORMS
or THERAPY

The can was bumping
with the force within.
Juicy wriggly worms
fighting for attention.

I took off the lid,
and took out a worm.
I held it up gently
And talked.

Then I put him down
On the Earth.
He wriggled
and then made a dive
under the grass,
into the mud.

I did this with several.
Separately, each.

Then out of the can
came a singing sound,
and as I watched
a rainbow light flickered
and glowed from it.

I knew
there were still worms there.
But the light
was wonderful to watch.

Charmian Goldwyn

COTTON WOOL

Cotton wool fills my head:
I suppose it must be the pills.
The world still looks quite fuzzy ahead:
Agreeably soft, but no thrills.

Life runs rough revolutions
To bruise my sensitive brain,
But the packaging round the convolutions
Dulls the worst of the pain.

If my brain grows a thicker skin,
Will it still let the wonder in?

Ray Hume

NAMING THE BEAST

Their impression:
it's depression.
It sounds absurd,
that feeble word
which names my ill.
I'm trying to still
the surging flood
of boiling blood
searing my heart,
ripping apart
and burning a hole
to drain my soul
of all that I am:
a slaughtered lamb,
burnt and bad.
Very mad.

Ray Hume

TO MAKE MY WALL

Today the stones know where to go
they fall into their place first time
new neighbours fitting in along my line
ready to settle for a while
to make my wall

Yesterday was different I was left
with gaps and every one I picked up
failed to fit despite my turning each
around and over trying another
to make my wall

Today they seem to go together
one by one old stones square up
standing back I am surprised
that untidy pile has reassembled
to make my wall.

Richard Westcott

STROKE SOUNDS SUCH A SWEET WORD

STROKE sounds such a sweet word –
The open hand of loving kindness
Flows the length, smoothing and calming,
To produce a purr, perhaps,
And end in a kiss.

But *STRUCK* – the past participle
Percussive and to the point –
Is quite different, when stroke becomes
Smitten, the hand's a fist
And damage is done.

Richard Westcott

IMAGING

What's that blotch?
The patchy picture picks apart
the riddle in my middle.
I cough and splutter as you mutter.
What's packing out the pleura?
On the window to my insides
I see a smudge that looks benign
but you say it's a sign
that takes its toll upon my time.
That Rorschach chart of grey is mine
but I can't see me in those lines.

Alex Hillman
medical student

PROSTATE ANGER

A dark and private part of me
Hosts stark dark-centred cells free
To grow, divide, and wander: be
In places they've no right to be.

Since when perverse autonomy prevailed
I cannot know, since blood-tests failed
To show the start of rebellion veiled
With false reassurance: so I rail.

PSA *, you've let me down!
More nanograms needed to announce the noun:
Cancer – kept secret with a frown,
Till chance biopsy denounced you, clown.

I have no pain; I can pee for three,
But fear is a phantom teasing me:
Do I cut you, burn you, or wait and see?
Who will live longer, you or me?

I need to look inside my cell,
Then bolt - but bolt the door as well.

Ray Hume – 3rd June 2012

PSA - Prostate specific antigen

VIPER

She's timid but aggressive, with a body zigzagged green,
the beginning of a v-neck that forgot to peter out.
She's lounging on the very stone that's bathed in April sun,
on which, before, her parents used to coil in equal heat
to watch the darting world revealed to sleepers like themselves;
the very stone on which she'd been conceived not long ago.

Most country people know they should not touch a
    coiled-up snake,
not even with a fascinated, probing, prodding stick –
though hard to stay the hand when armed with
    such security,
the which can prove quite false in face of lightning
    fanged response.
Legs, or arms that are uncovered tend to take the brunt;
the result's the same – swelling, pain, collapse and
    sometimes death.

There's little John, for instance – spying one racing to a hole
to reach its place of safety in the dry stones of the dyke –
followed it with an instinctive hand too young to know
    the truth,
that adders under threat can only answer with a bite.
He sensed a shrill of pain he'd never felt the like before,
and saw his arm swell black within ten seconds of the sting.

But country doctors know of this emergency too well.
They know that if the duel with death's delayed too long
a healthy lad on thoughtless spree can lose the chance to live.

Good luck had Doctor Campbell on a visit to the farm.
He heard – and knew – the screams; raced far faster
  than he could;
gave the death-denying treatment that saved the
  youngster's life.

Chris Cameron

ATAXIA
or ARRIVAL OF FIRST GRANDSON

A winter's walk across the frozen grass,
up Yarrow, glinting in the angled light
that's borrowed from the Spring, a dream away,
that made us glad that day to be alive.

But I was dragging back, and couldn't match
John's usual stride, and blamed the winter's sloth,
or arrival of unwelcome sixty-five;
as if my clock could tell the time so well!

A lecture later, and my world began
to spin. I rose to go – was all at sea,
and tried, as Peter did, to walk the waves,
but lacked, like him, the necessary faith.

Then came a month of doctors' tests,
which though precise, not quite enough
to tell me what I needed most to know –
that I might live to tell the tale, or no.

New life gave hope when Owen Will arrived,
a lovely grandson – aren't they all?
His eyes met mine, and though my world
might stay disturbed, I knew I'd see him grow.

Chris Cameron

BREATHING BOTTLES

Three of them in the glass case
Looking as if they have been bashed about
Gently.

They look pale and I wonder if they can breathe
I want to touch them, I think they could help
Us.
For we have been knocked about too.

Or are we beyond help, those who wait,
The ceiling presses down, there's not quite enough
Air.

Can we touch the Breathing Bottles,
Mould them to the shape of our hand,
Breathe the balm to heal and soothe?

Teresa Black

Inspited by a seeing piece made by Jenny Pope from unglazed porcelain, on display in Bilston Craft Gallery, which also unintentionally evoked thoughts about asthma.

CHANCE MEETING

"Hi, it's me!"
A voice called in the street
"Remember me?
You looked after me.
I want to thank you."
He had been my patient.
All alone in this country
Fleeing from torture and oppression
For expressing his opinion
His body slowly healed.
The healing of his mind
Took much longer.
In those days,
I was all he had.
The only one to care.
He looked much younger.
Years of grief and pain
Used to cloud his face.
Now he looked hopeful and free.
We exchanged numbers
But I won't hear from him again.
I walked away.
It was dusk.
The sky was grey with drizzle.
But for me, the sun shone.

Chris Walker

ON WRITING A MEDICO-LEGAL REPORT
or AN ASYLUM SEEKER'S HISTORY

I poised with my fingers over the keys . . .
'History' said the title.
History of this man's torture,
his humiliation, his pain.
My fiftieth case. I paused again.
I didn't want to write again.
Man's inhumanity to man appalls me.
The arbitrariness of torture
For what gain?
Little boys pull off insects' wings.

'History'.
He was born there and spoke thus,
Looked different,
Worshipped another God.

He said,
The Others wanted me elsewhere, or dead.
Meanwhile they used me. For sport.

They said,
Cigarette burns, that's fun.
Hang him upside down.
Doesn't he look cool?
Like the dog I threw stones at,
he cringes, cries out, yelps
like a cur. Let us show him who is king!
I'm the King of the castle . . .

And someone's life is ruined,
casually, by thugs.

Charmian Goldwyn
75

JESUS IN AN IMMIGRATION COURT

If Christ would show his palms
the Judge would say,
"I think these scars
are self-inflicted."

Charmian Goldwyn

TEREZÍN TRANSIT CAMP

There are no butterflies at Terezín
symbols of freedom, with eccentric flight
leaving barrier and barbed wire behind.

The children draw them anyway.
Forgetting hunger, sickness, crowding, hell,
they fly over walls towards the sun.

Painting scenes of Ghetto home,
carts, horses, parents, friends, no longer there.
Their palettes darken.
People sit in hunched despair.
The lonely sign 'To Prague' has disappeared.
Black clouds fill the sky.

These little artists died, bearing
the hopeful spirit of the young.

Charmian Goldwyn

Author's note: Terezín was the transit camp for Jews, kept as a show case for the Red Cross, but in fact thousands died there of malnutrition, and thousands more were shipped on to the death camps. Whist they were there, the children were taught secretly to draw and paint. Their pictures survive and are exhibited in Prague and at Terezín, now a memorial.

I MARCH WITH THOUSANDS

I march with thousands of others
Carrying 'No War in Iraq' or 'Blair out'.
I send money to Land Mine Charities
And I wish George Bush up the spout.

Why can't I do something singular,
Draw attention to sad refugees,
Streak through a game at Twickenham
Stand on my head in cream cheese?

Why don't I shout out in public
(apart from 'Bravo' at a match)?
How can anyone know I'm a radical
If all I can do is write crap?

Charmian Goldwyn

THE AMPUTEES

Begging in the market place
They cannot work, missing limbs,
No prosthetics, just stumps
And begging tins

Some turn up their noses
Others drop in a coin or two
Life goes on but
The amputees just beg.

How could they do that?
Why did the rebels chop off arms and legs?
Destroy livelihoods
What did they hope to gain?

"Do you want a short sleeve?
Or a long sleeve?"
What a choice. Better dead
Many thought.

As Sierra Leone rebuilds itself
After years of destruction
People must face
Devastation.

Do they hate each other?
No, forgiveness is in the air
Or maybe
They are still too shocked for anger.

Dorothy Crowther

FROM A REFUGEE CAMP ON THE THAI - BURMA BORDER

I can barely see, but I know it is sunset.
And I am in the sunset of my life.
Not knowing what has happened
to my children, where they went
when SLORC * came and burnt our huts,
set mines and took me off
to labour for their army.
Are the children still living,
eating roots and berries in the jungle,
hiding from the guns?
Or are they lying in unmarked graves . . .

Somehow I escaped across the river
to the camp, and here I sit
and every day I hope
there will be news from them
and every day I pray
that there will be peace and resolution
in our land.

Charmian Goldwyn

---

*SLORC - Burmese Military State Law and Order Committee

THE WELL AT MAROUT

Children crush against me, small black bodies
almost smothered by the weight of others
trying to get close to the white woman,
the woman whose ancestors took
their ancestors for slaves.

Today I am the liberator.
The photo shows eager faces
dressed in their best for a rare event,
a life-changing occasion.
Behind us, the well, which I opened.

No longer will women carry water on their heads
for miles across the mangrove causeway
backs and necks aching
fear of slipping with each step.
Fresh water is here for all.

They sing in their native Krio
"Tenkee! Tenkee!" *
Thanks to this woman from overseas.
Thank you for your help
and for providing this well.

Then they take me to their beach
where the children play and swim,
an air of joy and festivity surrounds us,
not a care in the world.
Enjoyment and freedom. However . . .

---

*Tenkee - "Thank you".

. . .they have no electricity or sewerage,
little food, no health care or education
and life expectancy is low.
But today their faces glow
with pleasure and gratitude.

Dorothy Crowther

AN AFRICAN BIKE RIDE

The equator crossed twice in one day in the heat of the sun
The harmony of African voices and the banging of a
  Bantu drum
Tyres on gravel, gentle wind in the Acacia trees, Masai in
  red robes
The beauty of the Rift Valley over black cotton and dirt
  track roads

Mount Kenya, the Aberdare Mountains, beautiful views over
  high plains
Hyrax nocturnal shrieking, like a child screaming in pain
On the road, delightful smiling children, old man in second-
  hand suit and a hat
After a day in the saddle, one litre of Macallan's whisky
  downed by veteran cyclists in two hours flat

Heat from the road especially during a twelve kilometre climb
Of course in retrospect the experience was divine!
Healing power of *aloe vera*, saddle sore, cuts and grazes,
  tired legs
Hot shower beneath open skies, slumber in my thermarest bed

Relief at the sight of the landcruiser which meant a roadside
  stop, water, cereal bars
Whisky and jokes under the canopy of the African sky and stars
Hot sulphurs, steam fumaroles, pumice stone, and obsidian
  so black
We cycled over rocks, down gorges, through river beds and on
  dust track

Papyrus at Lake Naivasha, pelicans, fish eagles, storks
    and hippo
Locals on loaded-up fixed-wheel bicycles smile and
    say 'Jambo'
Excitement at seeing rhino, water buffalo, zebra and
    Thomson's gazelles
Children as herdsmen, the sound of goats, and cattle bells.

I think of teenagers with cancer for whom we'd done
    this ride
Of African children in gaily coloured school uniform at
    the roadside
The eight of us became a team, friendship and humour
    as we cycled on the track
The beauty of the Rift Valley
Africa once visited, you want to go back

Jim Brockbank

ROOKIE ON THE FLY

Cottonwood, golden against the blue New Mexico sky
The timeless San Juan lies ready for the game
Beneath the flowing waters its secrets lie
These aquatic players no fools, not ready to be claimed

Above the waterline respectful opponents wait and watch.
So patiently the line of temptation is cast.
Which threaded imitation will make the catch?
Will it be checkmate at last?

Many casts and mends have yet to be made
Rainbow, Cut-throat, Brown, not tempted by illusion.
Above the waterline many hopes will fade
Meticulous preparation scattered to confusion

Suddenly the graphite bends, a strike! The reel spools out
    the line
Skill and maybe some luck bring the feisty combatant to the
    landing net
Subtle eco-changes understood, illusion wins this time
A Rainbow after all, admired then gently returned to the
    water, with respect.

Jim Brockbank

DIVING AT PARADISE BEACH, KADADIRI, SULAWESI

Beneath the waves
the sea is not silent.
It is full of tiny noise;
the tickling clicking sounds
of stone on stone
and fish nibbling coral.

We are intruders
in Poseidon's Kingdom.
Geared up like ancient knights
with aqualung and BCD *
A short adventure only
breathing precious pressured air.
We watch our depth
Lest we should get
Rapture of the Deep;
or on ascent
let loose absorbed air
into our land locked bodies.

Thanks Neptune for the permit
to view fantastic sights . . .
Ferned coral back-lit by sun,
a myriad brilliant little fish,
colours dappled in descending rays.
A secret grotto lined
by brightly jeweled sponges

---

*BCD - Buoyancy Control Device. Worn by divers. You fill it with a bit of
air when you want to go up and empty it when you want to go down.*

A cloud of fish stream past
minds in unison
upon an unknown quest.

And lurking in the caves
and watching from the deep
reminders of our frail forms
stone fish, scorpions, snakes and sharks.

I float in the sea
like a bird hovering
let my eyes take the scene
leave my brain wondering.

Take nothing but pictures, leave no fin prints

Charmian Goldwyn

KATHMANDU

In the Land of Snows Eternal
Rain pours down for days unceasing
Monsoon clouds mask towering mountains;
Atmosphere as thick as treacle
Clothing soaked in thirty minutes.

Eyes cast down see muck and ferment,
Poverty, disease and moulder
Yet these rains refresh the rice-fields
Breathe life anew to little creatures:
Cicadas squeaking, darters flitting,
Lace-wings, fireflies, even damsels,
Insects feeding feathered hunters.

Lonely plaintive blue kingfisher
Crying out bereft and mournful
Draws my eyes to his brown puddle
'Neath the window of my study
He sweeps down; a frog is pinioned
Swift arrives his faithful soul-mate
True-loves share their slithy dinner.

Then I catch a waft of incense,
Looking up, I see a rainbow
Thunder-clouds lined now with silver
Startling white of egrets wheeling
Dancing kites of joyous children.

Higher still above the monsoon
Snow-peaks peeking shyly downwards
Promise, soothe, entice, renew me;
Ganesh Himal lifts my spirits
Lifts my spirits from the mud.

Jane Wilson-Howarth

SONG THRUSH AT THE LIGHTS

You sing. How can I hear you?
But I do.

Does anyone else hear
your song, pouring out
Over the traffic?

You must think it worthwhile,
and it is
Because someone has heard you.

Teresa Black

Author's note: heard at the busy junction of Bilston Road and Stow Heath Lane, Wolverhampton, 21st March 2012

GOING FOR GOLD

Race your heart
this morning,
hurdle for health,
jet javelins of joy
and put that heavy shot
somewhere else.

High jump over
your difficult self, cross
countryside, chase
the distant steeple
of a church, clear
the clear stream
with a trailing foot.

Run along the track
that crosses the moor,
past spectator sheep
in fleeces, no applause
but the odd clap
of thunder, no photos,
but flashes of lightning.

Unfurl the blue sky,
mount the rostrum
of the hill, receive gold
medal sun, feel light
and up there
and on top of things.

Chris Woods

MEXICAN RAVE

It happened one night in a Mexican bar:
Pedro the barman left the door ajar.
From outside in the street as the sun went down,
The song of cicadas and frogs couldn't drown
Loud snorting and grunting, sneezes and coughs
At the entry of Conchita, wet-nosed from her trough.
She wasn't the barmaid, but a suffering sow
Who'd come in for comfort if Pedro'd allow.
She was red as a chilli and twice as hot,
But shivered and sweated like a lobster-pot.
Tequila had put Pedro's brain in a fuddle,
And he thought Conchita ripe for a cuddle.
She bristled and squealed on a rug by the wall,
Pedro's amorous advances not nice at all.
She shook off her companion without much ado
And left him incubating a new kind of flu.

So please watch out for the Mexican wave:
But the Government will tell us who we can save.

Ray Hume

Author's note: As sung by Tammy Flo, Country & Western Singer.
First published on www.nhs247.com May 2009

THE A TO Z OF SUCCESS IN SURGERY

A is for Attitude, have some, not too much,
B is for Bleeding, again, just a touch;
C is for Courses, you'll need quite a few,
D for Divorces, you might need these too;
E is forEver, how long clinics last,
F is for Friends, a nice part of your past.
G is for Goals, aim high or you'll fade,
H is for Holes, just put down the spade;
I for Idiots Guide, the best type of book,
J is for Juniors - how young they now look;
K for your Kids, remember their names,
L for the Lawyers - so giving (with blame).
M is for Medicine, you'll forget it all,
N is for Nights - no escape from 'the call';
O is for Orifice, prepare to explore,
P is for Publishing, a necessary chore;
Q is for Quarrels - every unit has some,
R for Research, a pain in the bum.
S is for Scrubs - its not like the show,
T is for Trouble - find cover, stay low;
U is for Underling, that's you for some years,
V is for Vanity, competing with peers;
W for Wine - you should go to a class,
X is for Xenon, a light inert gas;
Y is for Yahoo mail, your inbox is full,
Z for zoologist, be that, it's more cool.

Andrew J Diver

CHOLESTEROL

Cholesterol of 5.2
really is too high for you.
The rules have changed
and the reading should be no more
than at the very most just 4.

Years ago a woman was said to cope
with a cholesterol of 7 or 8
especially if she was overweight.
But that has changed:
it needs to be reduced.

So here I'm giving you a list
of foods which are high risk.
Butter, cream, alcohol and salt
must be reduced or if you die
it will be your fault.

And so it is that my GP
takes extra special care of me.
But when I say "My arthritis, doc?"
It comes to him as quite a shock.

It seems to me that this poor fellow
of recent years has had to mellow,
suppress his own ideas and thoughts,
and *learn to do what others*
seem to think he ought.

Dorothy Crowther

WHEN I AM OLD

When I am old I shall not wear purple
but I'll do all those things Mother said not to

So first to France, to the beach at Cap d'Agde
where all my clothes I shall promptly discard
I will run naked across the hot sand
gambolling, shrieking, in the waves all day
with my pink and wrinkled old birthday suit
and all of the young and the so beautiful
will stop and stare and say "silly old fruit"
but they'll give me a cheer anyway

I'll ride like the wind on a brave stallion
clinging on tight, probably side-saddle
on fast motorbikes I will ride pillion
with handsome young men in black-studded leathers
to the pubs and clubs with the boys I will go
try my best to be 'blue' and all blokey
with the girls I'll get high on chilled Chardonnay
and then I'll sing Karaoke

I'll ski a black run, of course at midnight,
soar high like Eddie the Eagle in flight
and I shall have to get sexy with Rexy
after all, he says I'm perfection
he's been asking for ages, trying so hard
so I think we'll do it – without protection.

On a plane I will go, when I am ready
real cool, a parachute jump, the epitome
I'll stand in the doorway, I will be steady
you've seen them do it, they won't have to push me

I will wear all the gear Health and Safety afford
I'll step into the blue and I won't pull the cord.

Paula Lawrence

DNA INTERRUPTUS

My genome was wrongly coded
chain broken down the line
somewhere, a random occurrence
you say, nobody's fault
no malice, no evil intent
an impromptu pairing
produced the flaw that is me
I was just next in line

and if I should struggle, if I
twine, no matter, you say
only a small imperfection
you're doing just fine

but hey, doc, now that you've cracked it
now that you're so clever
don't rush, in your own time
rub me out. Try the new script

But please – get me right next time.

Paula Lawrence

SICK AS A PARROT

I think my parrot's got the flu,
And I haven't a clue what to do:
Shall I cool his head until he freezes,
And smack his back until he sneezes?

Paracetamol might ease his pain;
Encourage his croaky voice again.
I miss his raucous squawking and swearing:
Pleasing, teasing, daring, wearing.

I'll say he needs an antibiotic -
Shame if they think that I'm neurotic.
There's always the fear of secondary infection:
I *know* it's dear - but *give* him an injection!

I've suddenly had a terrible thought:
I'll *hide* his suffering - yes I *ought*:
They'll want to put him in quarantine,
Or put him down, quietly, and unseen.

       – And that's *no* way to treat a parrot.

Ray Hume

IT HURTS

"Doctor, when I lift my arm
The pain is what I dread."

"Well, then, try to avoid the harm
By keeping it still instead."

"Yes, but it hurts in all three places,
There, along the bone."

"Well, then, try to avoid those places –
Preferably stay at home."

Ray Hume

THE POEMS: AUTHOR INDEX

. . . author index continued

ACKNOWLEDGEMENTS

We, the editors, wish to thank everyone involved in preparing and producing this book; Tim Jones for expert proof-reading and helpful comments; Mike Walker for the cover illustration, and for being so creative and adaptable; RAP Spiderweb, our printers in Oldham, for being prompt and helpful throughout; The Chairman and Committee of the Society of Medical Writers, for useful information and advice; our families for their support; and the SOMW members who have generously contributed their poems.

Mary Anderson, Joanne Regan, Chris Walker. September 2012

SOCIETY OF MEDICAL WRITERS
APPLICATION FOR MEMBERSHIP

Please *copy and fill this application form, and return it with your fee to*
<u>Dr R Cutler 30 Dollis Hill Lane LONDON NW2 6JE</u>

I wish to apply for membership of S.O.M.W.
I enclose [_] my cheque for £___ or [_] a standing order form.
Cheques should be made payable payable to 'S.O.M.W.'
Annual membership: doctors £50.00; allied health professionals £30.00;
students £15.00

Title: *(Dr; Prof; etc.)*   **Surname:**
Forenames:
Address:

County: **Postcode:**

Website: if any

Home Tel:

Mobile:

e-mail:

Occupation and for how long:

Special interests
  Medical:

  Non-medical / or hobbies:

Are you prepared to speak?- Yes / No; **write?** - Yes / No;
  translate into other languages ? (Please specify which)- Yes / No.

Please give details, of your writing / speaking experience if any,
or mini profile or CV *(no more than 25 words)*.

Signed: **Dated:**